·uth

planet

by Richard Wilkinson and Kate Pickett

About the Friedrich-Ebert-Stiftung

The Friedrich-Ebert-Stiftung is a non-profit German political foundation committed to the advancement of public policy issues in the spirit of the basic values of social democracy through education, research, and international cooperation. The foundation, headquartered in Berlin and Bonn, has regional offices throughout Germany, maintains offices in over 90 countries and carries out activities in more than 100 countries.

Friedrich-Ebert-Stiftung
44 Charlotte Street, London W1T 2NR,
T: +44 (0)207 612 1900
E: info@feslondon.net
www.feslondon.org.uk

About the Authors

Richard Wilkinson has played a formative role in international research on the social determinants of health and on the societal effects of income inequality. He studied economic history at LSE before training in epidemiology. He is Professor Emeritus of Social Epidemiology at the University of Nottingham Medical School, Honorary Professor at UCL and a Visiting Professor at the University of York. Richard co-wrote *The Spirit Level* with Kate Pickett which won the 2011 Political Studies Association Publication of the Year Award and the 2010 Bristol Festival of Ideas Prize. Richard is also a co-founder of The Equality Trust.

Kate Pickett trained in biological anthropology at Cambridge, nutritional sciences at Cornell and epidemiology at UC-Berkeley, and is currently Professor of Epidemiology in the Department of Health Sciences at the University of York. She co-founder of The Equality Trust and is co-author of *The Spirit Level*, and fellow of the RSA. Her research focuses on the social determinants of health, particularly the influences of such factors as income inequality, social class, neighbourhood context and ethnic density on such varied outcomes as mortality and morbidity, teenage birth, violent crime, obesity, social mobility and health-related behaviours.

CONTENTS

Foreword   ix
Summary   xii
Introduction   1

1. The Big Picture   5

2. Equality and the Path to   13
Environmental Sustainability

3. A Countervailing Force   29

4. Spreading Economic Democracy   43

Conclusion   55

FOREWORD

Andrew Harrop and Ulrich Storck

As elections approach, politics often narrows in its focus. Vision tends to extend little beyond voters' doorsteps.

Of course political parties need to address people's immediate concerns, but they also have a duty to inspire: to make big arguments about how a particular political creed will address the world that's coming. In recent years the need for progressive political visions has often been proclaimed; but politics has remained reactive to day-to-day demands and preoccupied with small-scale policy.

This pamphlet not only reminds us of the negative impacts of rising inequality for the quality of our lives, it also shows how these are linked to one of the fundamental challenges facing humanity today: climate change. Global warming has been at the margins of both the British Labour party's intellectual debate in opposition; and the coalition's programme in government, despite prime minister David Cameron's pledge to lead "the greenest government ever". But, as Richard Wilkinson and Kate Pickett point out, "if we fail to reverse the policies that have been driving climate change, we face disaster on a world scale".

In *The Spirit Level*, the authors provided the left with the rigorous evidence base to support the claim we instinctively knew to be true – that inequality is socially corrosive and more equal societies do better across the board. In *A Convenient Truth* they guide us towards a future that is environmentally sustainable and that also maximises human wellbeing. Inequality drives status insecurity, which fuels the consumerism that is destroying our planet. But the things we buy aren't making us any happier: the link between economic development and real improvements in quality of life is broken in rich societies.

For real improvements in wellbeing, we need a more equal society, where community life can be restored, where people can look each other in the eye again, and we can enjoy the company of friends and family. As the authors note, "the most fundamental benefit of reducing the very large differences in income and wealth which disfigure many societies is the improvement in the quality of social relations and the increases in social cohesion".

Change on the scale the authors demand can't be achieved by income transfers. It needs equality to spread deep into the foundations of our society through economic democracy. Wilkinson and Pickett highlight existing examples, such as the compulsory representation of employees on boards in countries like Germany, which have contributed to a more democratic corporate life, and call for an expansion of co-ops and employee-owned companies. The introduction of a federal minimum wage in Germany this year or the 'living wage' campaign in the UK, constitute steps in the right direction. But fundamental change can only be embedded if democratic constraints are intrinsic features of the economic system. As Wilkinson and Pickett put it: "Rather than being a revolution, it is a gradual but vital transformation."

This is a pamphlet that provides a bold and optimistic vision of a better society, rooted in detailed evidence, with a series of practical policy steps for how to get there. It shows that the levels of inequality in society differ widely even within Europe. Countries could learn from each other and adopt measures that helped their neighbours to reduce inequality in their societies. G.D.H Cole – the great sage of industrial democracy – lamented that "We are too apt, despite our will to regenerate society, to regard the present character-istics…as fixed and unalterable". Wilkinson and Pickett offer us hope that politics can provide us with a different future and that the transition to environmental sustainability is not only within our grasp, but will be better for all of us.

Andrew Harrop is general secretary of the Fabian Society
Ulrich Storck is the director of the Friedrich-Ebert-Stiftung
in London

Summary

Although economic development is what has transformed the real quality of life during the last couple of centuries, in the rich countries it has largely finished its work. The evidence shows very clearly that, in the rich countries, economic growth no longer drives measures of either health or happiness, adult or child wellbeing.

But it is a remarkable coincidence that, just as this has become evident, we have also become aware of the environmental limits to growth. Though ignored by sceptics, the scientific evidence on the consequences of carbon emissions is incontrovertible.

Given our predicament, what is astonishing is that carbon emissions continue to rise and the world's politicians are nowhere near agreement on policies to make the necessary dramatic reductions. The explanation is that reducing carbon emissions is seen as an unwelcome belt-tightening exercise. Moving towards sustainability is regarded as a matter of reducing the environmental impact of our existing way of life.

This pamphlet shows another path. There are ways of moving towards environmental sustainability which would simultaneously bring real improvements in human wellbeing.

It is an important and extraordinarily convenient truth that, just as higher material standards have ceased to be critical to raising wellbeing in the rich countries, improving the quality of social life and the social environment has become crucial.

A growing body of research evidence makes it possible to track the deep sources of our society's social and psychological malaise to crisis levels of self-doubt and insecurity about how we are valued. As settled communities have disappeared, we encounter each other as socially exposed, unknown individuals, whose worth we judge substantially from social position. Outward wealth becomes the measure of inner worth, while status and social position are assumed to be indicators of intelligence and ability. The larger the income differences, the stronger the impression that some people are extremely important and others are almost worthless.

In a fragmented and atomised society, with status differences augmented by bigger material differences between people, we are inevitably more prone to status anxieties and worries about the impression we create in the minds of others. This feeds directly into consumerism as we try to communicate our 'worth' to each other by cloaking ourselves in the symbols of money, status and success. Inequality makes money even more important as a marker of what you are 'worth'.

Greater equality is then a key objective, not only because it reduces social dysfunction and improves health and wellbeing, but also because it makes it possible to overcome some of the main obstacles to sustainability. The most important of these is consumerism, which, driven by status competition, intensifies the demand for ever higher incomes and leads people to see sustainability simply as a threat to living standards.

Another link between greater equality and achieving sustainability comes from the fact that community life is much stronger in more equal societies and people are much more likely to feel they can trust each other. Populations become more public-spirited and have a stronger sense of the public good. If the modern world is to move towards an environmentally sustainable way of life, it means acting as never before on the basis of the common good, indeed the good of humanity as a whole.

To counter the take-off of top incomes which has been the main driver of increasing inequality, we need to build effective democratic constraints permanently into the economic system. If greater equality were to depend primarily on the redistribution of income, with pre-tax income differences undiminished, it would remain vulnerable. Redistribution through taxes and social security benefits can be undone at the stroke of any new government's pen. But increases in economic democracy ensure that greater equality is more deep-seated in the fabric of society.

In order to achieve this, the democratisation of the economy needs to be a publicly recognised political objective, advocated and defended by all progressive politicians as the next major step in human emancipation. We need to create a popular understanding that this is part of a transition to a sustainable future capable of achieving a higher quality of life than is now possible. Rather than being a revolution, it is a gradual but vital transformation which should include the following steps:

- **Require, by law, that all except the smallest companies** should have employee representatives on company boards and remuneration committees. The proportion of employees on these bodies should be higher in companies with larger numbers of employees.
- **The proportions of employee representatives on** company boards and remuneration committees should be set to increase over time, moving eventually to majority control and beyond. This could be achieved by requiring that a small proportion of shares be transferred each year to employee-controlled trusts.
- **Before making either of these a legal requirement,** conformity with provisions such as these could be made a condition of gaining public sector contracts or lower corporation tax rates.
- **A major obstacle to the development of this sector is** the lack of knowledge of these models among professional legal and financial advisers. The Department for Business, Innovation and Skills should promote a single route to employee ownership and establish the necessary

legislative support. The department should also provide a training and advice service on how to set up employee owned and co-operative companies.

- **A government should work out a complete package of** measures to grow the democratic sector, complete with tax incentives, sources of advice and support, ready-made rules of governance and sources of finance.
- **The constitutions of employee-owned and co-operative** business should in all cases be designed to prevent employees selling their companies back to external shareholders.
- **Employees taking on new roles on company boards** would need a variety of options for training in areas such as management, business law, accountancy and economics. Options should range from some of the learning schemes designed to prepare school governors, to the provision of master's degrees to which people could be seconded
- **Set up an internet portal to help people to do their** shopping from democratic businesses and introduce a 'democratic company' logo, modelled on the 'fair trade' example, to increase the visibility of these companies.

What matters most for reducing inequality is the strength of progressive politics as a countervailing voice in society. Sometime after the late 1970s the political left lost its conviction that a better form of society was possible and left the way open for the rise of neoliberalism. It is now urgent that progressive forces in society should clarify an inspiring view of a future society which is not only environmentally sustainable, but in which the real quality of life is better for the vast majority.

INTRODUCTION

Since the 1980s, progressive politics has been rudderless. Having lost its vision of how to create a qualitatively better society for everyone, radical politics has lacked idealism, a sense of purpose and the ability to inspire. As a result, politicians seem driven mainly by short-term expediency, and great swathes of the population regard politics as not worth thinking about.

But there has never been such a crying need for a bold vision of the future. If we fail to reverse the policies that have been driving climate change, we face disaster on a world scale. Adverse trends have been visible for some time, the direction of change is beyond doubt and the main causes are understood.

Yet most of us shut our eyes to the problem. Moving towards sustainability looks like nothing so much as an unwelcome invitation to live in an impoverished version of our current reality. With the exception of more efficient new technology which saves us money, reductions in carbon emissions are seen as threatening many of the pleasures in life – from holiday flights to air conditioning. The environmental policies which we need have little chance of gaining popular support in societies dominated by consumerism, in which success means getting richer, and in which we are all manipulated by corporations hell bent on profit and expansion regardless of the consequences. We clearly need to find another approach.

Part of what blinds us to alternatives is that we see rich, developed societies as the peak of human achievement. But the truth is that, despite historically unprecedented levels of comfort and plenty, our societies have many serious social failings and are not efficient producers of wellbeing. People experience much of life as stressful and many, particularly teenagers and young adults, are dogged by self-doubt and low self-esteem. Each year about a quarter of all British adults suffer some form of mental illness – particularly depression, anxiety disorders, and drug or alcohol addiction. Our prisons are full and overcrowded. Children face high rates of bullying at school. Self-harm – particularly among teenage girls – is rife. Low social mobility means that children's life chances, far from being equal, are marked by major injustices. And, although research on both health and happiness shows the crucial importance of a fulfilling social life, community life in most areas varies between poor and non-existent. Many people feel isolated and most do not feel that the pleasure of spending free time with a group of friends is there for the taking.

So the task for everyone with any concern for the current and future welfare of humanity, is to think through how we can combine sustainable economic systems with genuinely higher levels of wellbeing.

This task is less difficult than you might expect. The key, as this pamphlet will show, is that the wellbeing of populations in the rich societies now depends less on further advances in material standards than on improving the quality of social relations and community life. Improvements in health, happiness and other measures of adult or child wellbeing are no longer linked to economic growth.

A growing body of research evidence makes it possible to track the deep sources of our society's social and psychological malaise to crisis levels of self-doubt and insecurity about how we are valued. As settled communities have disappeared, we encounter each other as socially exposed, unknown individuals, whose worth we judge substantially from social position. Outward wealth becomes the measure of inner worth, while status and social position are assumed to be indicators of intelligence and ability. The effect is that bigger inequalities in material circumstances – in housing, cars, jobs, education – create bigger differences in social worth and bigger social distances. The larger the income differences, the stronger the impression that some people are extremely important and others are almost worthless.

What this means is that the greater the inequality, the more stressful social contact will seem and the more people will start to withdraw from community life. A great deal of research now testifies to the strong connection between societies having larger income differences and weaker community life. Indeed, the most fundamental benefit of reducing the very large differences in income and wealth which disfigure many societies is the improvement in the quality of social relations and the increases in social cohesion.

Because smaller income differences reduce the importance of status differences, they also reduce the consumerism which status insecurity intensifies. This is especially important because consumerism is such a major obstacle to sustainability. From the perspective of both human wellbeing and the environment, we have to replace socially and environmentally destructive status competition with the more affiliative social relations and community life which human wellbeing requires.

How then, can income and status differences be reduced? There is, as we will show, ample evidence that the big changes in inequality reflect the shifting balance of political and ideological forces in societies rather than changes in impersonal market forces. We argue that the best way of building more equal and sustainable societies is to extend democracy into the economic sphere, so making income differences within organisations more sensitive to democratic pressures.

Where ranking systems and status divisions are strongest, and where the biggest income differences are created, is in business – particularly in large private sector corporations. If you look at the studies comparing different business models, it turns out that more democratic models tend to have higher productivity. They also tend to be more congenial places to work. This is true of companies with employee representatives on the board (a legal requirement in many European countries) as well as of companies which are either employee co-operatives or fully employee-owned. More democratic companies typically have much smaller pay differences within them. For this and a number of other reasons, we believe that they may provide the best foundation on which to create a permanently more equal and sustainable society. Indeed, we see the extension of democracy into economic institutions as the next major step in the long project of human emancipation

1: THE BIG PICTURE

The developed countries have reached a major turning point in human history. Although economic development is what has transformed the real quality of life during the last couple of centuries, in the rich countries it has largely finished its work. The evidence shows very clearly that in the rich countries economic growth no longer drives measures of wellbeing.

As an example, Figure 1 shows the relation between life expectancy and national income per head for countries at all stages in economic development. It shows that life expectancy rises rapidly in the early stages of economic growth and then gradually levels out until, among the richest countries, the relationship becomes horizontal and any connection is lost.

This is not a 'ceiling effect' as we reach the limits of human life expectancy. That can be ruled out because longevity is continuing to rise as fast as it did during other periods over the last century: we still gain two to three years of life expectancy with every decade that passes. What has happened is that the relationship between life expectancy and economic growth has been broken. Even when you look at changes over periods of time as long as 40 years, there is little or no correlation between national income per head and life expectancy.[1]

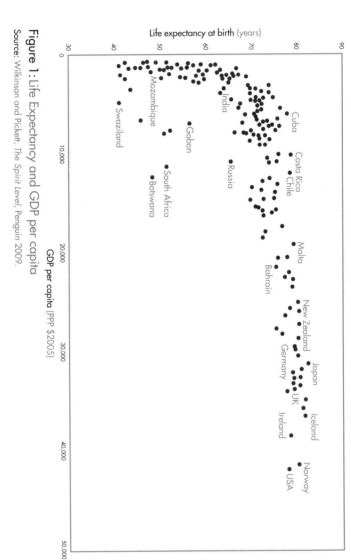

Figure 1: Life Expectancy and GDP per capita
Source: Wilkinson and Pickett, *The Spirit Level*, Penguin 2009.

Very similar patterns can be seen if you look at measures of happiness and wellbeing – rapid rises in the early stages of economic development are followed by a levelling out as countries get richer. What the data is telling us is a simple but fundamental truth: that for people in less developed countries, where many do not have access to basic necessities, economic development and rising material standards remain important drivers of wellbeing. But for people in the rich countries, having more and more of everything makes less and less difference.

Essentially this is a process of diminishing returns to increases in income which would inevitably appear at some point in the long course of economic development. Having more makes a bigger difference to those who have least.

At the same time, environmentalists have shown in one developed country after another, that measures of economic welfare – which, like the Genuine Progress Indicator, subtract the many negatives (like car crashes and costs of air pollution) from national income – no longer rise with national income per head. But it is important to remember that, even if economic growth had fewer negative consequences, this would not mean that economic growth would continue to increase levels of wellbeing for us as it did for previous generations. The limit to increased human wellbeing from continued rises in income is more fundamental than that.

The environmental limits of growth

It is a remarkable coincidence that, just as it has become evident that economic growth has largely finished its work in transforming the quality of human life in the rich countries, we have also become aware of the environmental limits to growth. Though ignored by sceptics, the scientific evidence on the consequences of carbon emissions is incontrovertible.

In May 2013, carbon concentrations in the atmosphere (measured at Mauna Loa in the middle of the Pacific to avoid the influence of local pollution) surpassed 400 parts per million (ppm) for the first time. That is 40 per cent higher than before industrialisation – and higher than humans have ever breathed before.

For those who find it hard to imagine how human activity can change the climate, it is worth remembering that if you take a desktop model of the globe one foot in diameter, 95 per cent of the atmosphere would lie within a layer round it of only about a quarter of the thickness of a credit card.

The separate contributions to the increased carbon in the atmosphere from each of the main sources – the use of oil, coal and natural gas, from forest clearance and cement production – are well known; and global warming is a predicted and inescapable consequence of rising levels of carbon dioxide and other greenhouse gasses which allow the sun's rays in, but prevent some of the heat they generate escaping back into space. Meticulously plotted graphs from key agencies such as NASA show CO_2 concentrations and global average temperatures rising almost in lock-step. Others show the rapid decline in the polar ice-caps and the rise in sea levels.

In 2007, James Hansen (head of NASA's Goddard Institute of Space Studies) and an international scientific team estimated that 350ppm was the safe limit for atmospheric CO_2 concentrations if we are to keep the rise in global temperatures below 2C.[2] However, it is now clear the 1C rise in global temperatures which has already taken place is having consequences more like what had been predicted for 2C.

It looks now as if there is no 'safe' limit to the rise in global temperatures which can be tolerated. In 2009, the Geneva-based Global Humanitarian Forum, presided over by Kofi Annan, estimated that, through heatwaves, drought, water shortages and flooding, climate change was already causing 300,000 deaths a year and that there were already 26 million people displaced by climate change. This figure is thought likely to triple by the 2020s. Ninety per cent of the deaths were in developing countries rather than in the rich countries which have the highest carbon emissions per head. The annual number of deaths was predicted to rise to 500,000 a year by 2030.

Global warming is proceeding more rapidly than previously thought. In addition, some of the effects already set in train by higher CO_2 levels take long periods of time to come through, so that even if we immediately stopped further increases in CO_2 emissions, sea level rises (currently increasing at a rate of around 3mm per year) and climate change will continue into the distant future.[3] It is estimated that to stabilise atmospheric concentrations of CO_2 the carbon emissions caused by global human activity would have to be reduced by 80 per cent on 1990 levels.[4]

The environmental crisis is, however, more than climate change. As Clive Spash points out, it is also soil erosion, deforestation, water salinisation, the systemic effects of insecticides and pesticides, toxic chemical waste, species loss, acidification of the oceans, decline of fish stocks, hormone discharges into the water supply, and so on.[5]

However, the failure to reduce carbon emissions means that many climate scientists believe that we will soon be locked into the devastating consequences of 4C of global warming by 2060 – when present-day school children reach middle age. Given our predicament, what is astonishing is that carbon emissions continue to rise and, despite the scientific evidence, the world's politicians are nowhere near agreement on policies to make the necessary dramatic reductions.

The explanation is that reducing carbon emissions is seen as an unwelcome belt-tightening exercise. In most people's minds it would mean policies such as carbon taxes and reduction in levels of consumption which would threaten our incomes and material standards. The problem is seen as one of preserving lifestyles as far as possible in the face of the threatening implications of climate science. Moving towards sustainability is regarded as a matter of reducing the environmental impact of our existing way of life. Hence, new technologies such as low emission car engines and environmentally-friendly light bulbs are welcomed only if they reduce costs and so increase our real incomes.

The proper response to this situation is to think whether there are ways of moving towards environmental sustainability which would simultaneously bring real improvements in human wellbeing. The question of how we can make further improvements in human wellbeing is also posed by the evidence we have discussed showing that economic growth no longer improves wellbeing in the richest countries. Do our societies and way of life really mark the summit of human wellbeing or are there new avenues of human progress to be explored?

The future we need

For the political left, socialism was a conception of a society which would produce a qualitatively better way of life for the vast majority. It was an ideal that inspired many to devote their lives to gaining political change. However, we know what happened to the socialist experiment – the problems which led to restrictions on freedom and democracy, the inefficiency of state planning and the way governments felt it necessary to protect themselves with secret police.

But there has never been a more important time to look at what possibilities the future might offer us. This is not only because of the need to move towards sustainability, the uncoupling of growth and wellbeing, or because – as environmentalists point out – 'business as usual' is no longer a viable policy for the future. In addition, globalisation is part of a more fundamental long-term transition from the agricultural self-sufficiency of peasant farmers to a system of world interdependence, in which we depend for our food, clothing, technology and information on an integrated worldwide network of production, consumption and electronic communication. This coming together of the human race to form what amounts to a global organism has been likened to the transition from single celled organisms to the formation of multicellular organisms.[6]

Linked to that, our species, which originally emerged from Africa and diversified as it spread across the world, is now coming together again. Through international travel, migration and intermarriage, we are seeing a process which amounts to nothing less than the reunification of the human race. It might cause friction from time to time, and there are of course some who try to put the clock back, but as a step in human development, the long-term result is both inspiring and completely unstoppable.

And lastly, the pace of technical change continues to accelerate. The seemingly endless innovations coming from areas such as electronics, bio-engineering and nanotechnology reconfigure the ground on which our way of life is built. Used wisely, technical innovation should expand our possibilities, making our societies and way of life more adaptable.

It would be easy to imagine that the more change there is – technical, environmental or our increasing worldwide interdependence – the harder it would be to think usefully about the future. But the truth is that the more change there is, the more important it is to have a clear idea of where you want to get to. A boat in a rough sea is continuously knocked off course and so the helmsman has much more to do than when sailing in calm water. As our societies are tossed about by changes which, left to themselves, may threaten human survival, it becomes crucial to have a clear idea both of the conditions which need to be met to ensure human wellbeing and of the kind of society we should be moving towards to achieve them.

2: EQUALITY AND THE PATH TO ENVIRONMENTAL SUSTAINABILITY

Partly in recognition of the fact that gross national product (GNP) per head can no longer be regarded as even an approximate measure of a population's wellbeing, governments have shown an increasing interest in augmenting it with measures of both objective and subjective wellbeing, including health, education and happiness. But merely measuring health or happiness does not tell us what their determinants are, or what policies will improve them.

If we are to understand the determinants of health and happiness, the first issue to clarify is the contrast between how they are related to income differences *within* societies but not to income differences *between* rich societies. The contrast can be seen very clearly if we look just at the data for the rich countries which were shown earlier in Figure 1. They are presented on their own in Figure 2.

Countries like the USA and Norway are twice as rich as countries like Greece, Israel and Portugal but levels of national income per head have no consequences for life expectancy. There is no suggestion of a relationship between the two. Contrast this with the very close relationship between life expectancy and income within societies shown in Figure 3. It shows small neighbourhoods (electoral wards) in England and Wales, classified by deprivation.

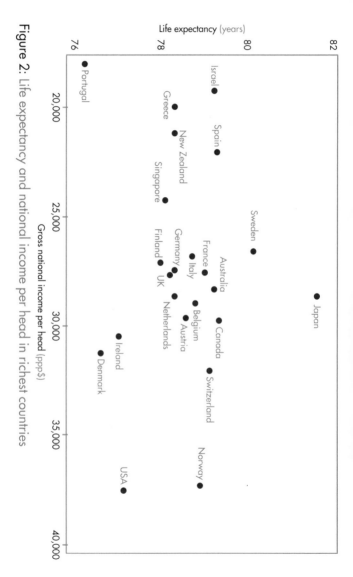

Figure 2: Life expectancy and national income per head in richest countries

The relationship is almost perfectly graded right across society. Health improves with each step up the socioeconomic scale. This is the pattern of health inequalities which can be seen in almost any society when health is shown arranged by income, education or any other indicator of socioeconomic status.

But the question here is why should health be so closely related to income within societies, but not at all to the income differences between rich societies? In other words, why the contrast between Figures 2 and 3? This is an important question because the same contrast is not confined to health. Richard Easterlin showed that it is also true of happiness.[7, 8, 9] The explanation of this paradox is that within societies we are looking at the effects of *relative* income and social status, at where we are on the social ladder compared to others in society. As soon as we recognise that what matters is relative income and status, the question that arises is what happens when the income differences between people – between rich and poor – get larger or smaller. This is the issue we investigated in our book *The Spirit Level*.[10] Basing our work on the research from round the world which has accumulated over the last 35 years, we showed that a wide range of health and social problems – including infant mortality, mental illness, violence, teenage births, imprisonment, child wellbeing, obesity, young people's maths and literacy scores and social cohesion – are all worse in societies in which income differences are bigger. We tested this not only among rich developed countries, but also, to provide a separate test bed, among the 50 states of the USA. We found that each of these problems was significantly related to inequality in both settings. The picture has been significantly strengthened more recently, showing the effects of inequality are both widespread and causal.[11, 12, 13]

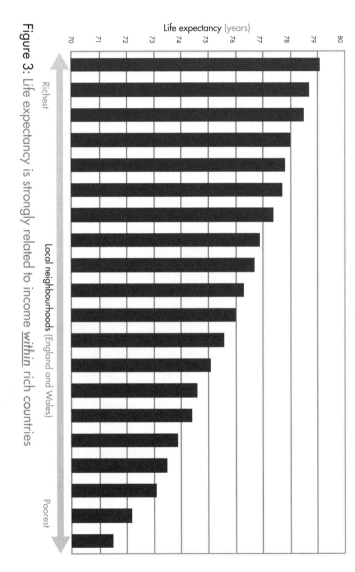

Figure 3: Life expectancy is strongly related to income *within* rich countries

Life expectancy (years)

Richest

Local neighbourhoods (England and Wales)

Poorest

Social status

People are sometimes surprised that so many, apparently quite different, health and social problems are all worse in more unequal countries. The explanation is that they are all problems related to social status, becoming more common lower down the social ladder. So what we are seeing is simply that problems related to social status within societies get worse if social status differences are increased. What is surprising, however, is that greater inequality seems to make them more common across the whole social spectrum. Although it makes most difference to the least well off, living in a more equal society seems to confer some advantage even on well-educated people with good jobs and incomes.

Two separate pieces of evidence make this clear. First, in a number of studies it is possible to compare people between more and less equal societies at each point in the social hierarchy, classified by incomes or educational level. Those studies provide a fairly consistent picture, suggesting that the biggest effects of inequality are lower down the social scale and get progressively smaller as you move towards the top of the hierarchy. When colleagues at the Harvard School of Public Health found how far up the income scale the effects of inequality went, they likened them to a form of 'pollution'.[14] The explanation seems to be that inequality changes the whole social fabric, increasing status competition and reducing trust and social cohesion right across societies.

The second reason for thinking that inequality does not just affect the poor, is that the differences in performance between more and less equal societies are much too large to be attributed to a poor minority alone. The health and social problems we looked at are all between twice as common and 10 times as common in more unequal societies. That the differences are so large is simply because we are all affected.

This fact helps us explain why so many health and social problems become more common at each step down the social ladder. The most common view is that social mobility represents a kind of sorting processes, so that people who are more vulnerable to ill health, drug problems, violence or mental illness, end up moving down the social ladder. But sorting people would not, in itself, make any characteristic more or less common in the population as a whole. That these problems are more common in societies with bigger income differences implies that they are substantially responses to social status differentiation itself. In other words, rather than thinking that a given proportion of the population have some vulnerability to physical or mental illness, to drug addiction or to violence, and that they drift downwards in society, the dramatic effects of more inequality on overall rates of these problems in society shows that it is the extent of status differentiation itself which makes these problems more common. These problems have to be understood not as a reflection of some imagined weakness of people lower on the status ladder, but as common effects which low social status has on human beings. Indeed they seem to be evolved responses to low social status which are part of all of us.

We are all affected by income differences more intimately than we realise. Living in a society where some people are very highly valued and seem so important, while others are regarded as almost worthless, makes us all more worried about how we are valued, whether we are respected or regarded as inferior. Inequality increases what psychologists have called the *'social evaluative threat'* – our worries about how others judge us. By increasing status competition and status insecurity, a society with bigger income differences increases all the problems to do with self-confidence and low self-esteem. That is almost certainly why societies with bigger income differences between rich and poor are less cohesive and have weaker community life. The increased social evaluative threat means that people start to feel that social contact is more of an ordeal than a relaxing and pleasurable experience.

There are two, almost opposite, responses to increased worries about social evaluations. One is an increase in social anxiety, lack of confidence, low self-esteem and depression, as people succumb to feelings of inferiority. The other, very different, reaction is a kind of self-aggrandisement and narcissism, as people try to present a positive view of themselves. Instead of being modest about their achievements and abilities, they start to flaunt and exaggerate them, talking themselves up, almost as a kind of self-advertisement.

The data shows both these patterns in action. People in more unequal societies suffer more status anxiety at all levels in the social hierarchy. They also have higher rates of depression and suffer more from other mental illnesses.[16, 17, 18] In addition, American data shows that narcissism rose during the 1980s and 1990s when income differences increased most rapidly.[19] And people go in for more of what psychologists call 'self-enhancement' in more unequal societies. When an international team asked people to rate themselves on a number of positive criteria, a much higher proportion of those in more unequal societies thought they were better than their national average.[20] Perhaps this is why a much larger majority of Americans than Swedes think they are better drivers than average. Social anxiety and self-enhancement are both understandable responses to an increased social evaluative threat.

Our human sensitivity to these kinds of worries was demonstrated very clearly in a study which assessed stress responses among people exposed to a range of different tasks and situations. Sally Dickerson and Margaret Kemeny, two psychologists at the University of California, Los Angeles, put together the data from over 200 studies in which volunteers had their levels of stress hormones measured while they performed various tasks deigned to be stressful. These studies were set up by psychologists trying to understand how we are affected by stress. Different experiments used different ways of inducing stress in volunteers. For example, some were asked to do mathematical problems; others to write about an unpleasant experience they had, and still others were videoed while doing things. Dickerson and Kemeny went through the results gleaned from all these different studies to see what kinds of task most reliably increased levels of the central stress hormone cortisol (measured in saliva or blood). Their conclusion was that we are particularly sensitive to "tasks that include social-evaluative threat … threats to self-esteem or social status, in which others could negatively judge performance".[21]

In short, we worry about how others judge us – afraid of making fools of ourselves or doing anything which would make others think less of us – and we easily become self-conscious and feel awkward if we fear being seen negatively. It is these kinds of social anxieties which lead people to withdraw from social life in societies with more inequality, and explain why greater inequality is associated with weaker community life. It also explains why violence (as measured by murder rates) has repeatedly been shown to be more common in more unequal societies.[22] The link is that where we judge each other more by status, people become more sensitive to loss of status and to the common triggers of violence such as disrespect, humiliation and loss of face. The tragedy is that by exacerbating all the effects of status insecurity, inequality cuts us off from the human company, friendship and community life, which ought to be a major part of our wellbeing and happiness.

Community life and the importance of social relationships

We showed earlier that the rich countries have largely come to the end of the real benefits which economic growth can bring to human wellbeing. If we are to continue to raise standards of wellbeing, we now have to look beyond economic growth. But just when material standards have ceased to be critical constraints on wellbeing, so the quality of social relationships and the social environment have become critical.

Just as it once took studies of crude outcomes like weight gain to show that, as well as feeding, babies also need loving contact and interaction with a parent, it looks as if it now takes studies of death rates to remind us of the social needs of adults. At some level we all know that wellbeing depends on social relationships, on friendship, on everything from close relationships to the quality of community life. A study which combined the data from 148 studies of friendship and health found that whether or not you have good friendship networks is at least as important to survival in a follow-up period as whether or not you smoke.[23] Experiments in which volunteers have been given a measured exposure to common cold viruses found that people with fewer friends were four times as likely to catch colds.[24] Other experiments have shown that wounds heal faster among those who have a good relationship with their partner.[25] The causal processes centre on the biology of stress and our sensitivity to the quality of relationships: good relationships are relaxing and bad relationships or isolation are very stressful.

Unsurprisingly, a large body of research shows that the quality of social relationships is also essential for human happiness and wellbeing.[26, 27] The richness of our social connections, from intimate relationships to friendship and the strength of community life more widely, have all been shown to make important contributions. A study using three sets of survey data, an international one, another for the USA, and one for Canada found that "marriage and family, ties to friends and neighbours, workplace ties, civic engagement (both individually and collectively), trustworthiness and trust: all appear independently and robustly related to happiness and life satisfaction".[28] Findings such as these are now plentiful and, since Richard Layard's book on *Happiness* in 2005, they are now more widely recognised.[29]

The importance of social relationships is, again, a truth that at some level we knew anyway, even without the benefit of research. Few are unaware that one of the most common traumatic experiences is the emotional impact of the break-up of a close relationship, and of course when a child comes home after a first day at a new school, the first question a parent will ask is "did you make friends?"

It is an important and extraordinarily convenient truth that, just as higher material standards have ceased to be critical to raising wellbeing in the rich countries, improving the quality of social life and the social environment has become crucial. The reasons why social life is, as we have seen, now critical are easy to see. The communities in which older people grew up were still remarkably stable. But during the last 50 years or so, geographical mobility has meant that people no longer remain in the same neighbourhoods, towns or cities in which they grew up, knowing many people for long spans of their lives. Not only has community life suffered as a result, but so have family relationships. After leaving home, people have less contact with parents and siblings than they used to, and contact with uncles, aunts and cousins is often confined to weddings and funerals. Increases in geographical mobility have also made it harder to keep up with former school friends. No longer surrounded by – and knowing ourselves through – long-term social relationships, we have become more vulnerable to worries about how we are seen and judged, whether by passing acquaintances or complete strangers.

Inequality and sustainability

In a fragmented and atomised society, with status differences augmented by bigger material differences between people, we are inevitably more prone to status anxieties and worries about the impression we create in the minds of others. This feeds directly into consumerism as we try to communicate our 'worth' to each other by cloaking ourselves in the symbols of money, status and success. Inequality makes money even more important as a marker of what you are 'worth'. As a result, people in more unequal societies work longer hours,[30] save less and get into debt more.[31, 32] As has been seen, international research shows that where income differences are wider there is more status insecurity right across society.[33, 34] As we use outward wealth as a measure of inner worth and judge each other more by status, money inevitably becomes more important as a means of showing your value.

Consumerism is not as happy an activity as the advertisers would have us believe. Rather than being associated with wellbeing, psychological studies suggest that it is driven by status insecurity. A recent survey of the findings of over 250 studies of wellbeing and whether people had a 'materialistic' and consumerist orientation found "a clear, consistent negative association between a broad array of types of personal wellbeing and people's belief in, and prioritization of, materialistic pursuits in life."[34] The connection between materialism and lower wellbeing seemed to involve "negative self-appraisals" as well as "low levels of satisfaction of needs for autonomy, competence, and relatedness". The evidence also shows that those who get into serious personal debt, particularly those who use pawnbrokers and moneylenders, suffer high rates of common mental disorders.[35] Informed by large numbers of studies in the research journals serving the marketing and fashion industries, advertisers exploit the links between status insecurity and consumerism relentlessly. Greater equality is then a key objective, not only because it reduces social dysfunction and improves health and wellbeing, but also because it makes it possible to overcome some of the main obstacles to sustainability. The most important of these is consumerism, which, driven by status competition, intensifies the demand for ever higher incomes and leads people to see sustainability simply as a threat to living standards.

Status competition is of course a zero sum game. We cannot all improve our status in relation to each other: one person's gain is another's loss. So although increases in *individual* income improve wellbeing if they move you up the social ladder, if everyone gets better off together it does nothing to improve overall wellbeing. In the rich countries it is therefore (as the contrast between Figures 2 and 3 makes clear) no longer legitimate to think that our individual desires for higher income can be satisfied by economic growth.

Another link between greater equality and achieving sustainability comes from the fact that community life is so much stronger in more equal societies and people are much more likely to feel they can trust others. This means that people are more public spirited and have a stronger sense of the public good. Research again shows that people in more unequal societies are less inclined to help others – the elderly, those with disabilities or anyone else.[36] In effect, greater inequality decreases reciprocity and makes people more out for themselves – regardless of others. If the modern world is to move towards an environmentally sustainable way of life, it means acting as never before on the basis of the common good, indeed the good of humanity as a whole.

There are already signs of the way greater equality can lead, via an increased awareness of the common good, towards sustainability. An international survey of the opinions of business leaders included a question about the priority they accorded to international environmental protection agreements.[37] As Figure 4 shows, business leaders in more equal countries rate environmental agreements as much more important than do business leaders in more unequal countries. Figure 5 shows the same pattern in recycling: more equal societies recycle a higher proportion of their different waste materials. Both these figures are indications that people in more equal societies are indeed less out for themselves and more willing to act for the common good.

These processes have something in common with the reasons why researchers, using a mathematical model of Human and Natural Dynamics (HANDY), found that when societies were faced with environmental resource scarcities, those divided by large economic inequalities were much more at risk of collapse than were more equal societies.[38]

Consumerism is the greatest obstacle to any attempt to reduce carbon emissions and move towards sustainability. Because it is driven by the status insecurities and status competition which bigger income differences intensify, any realistic attempt to rein in consumerism has to start by reducing income differences. Substantial reductions in income differences are however, not only central if we are to move towards sustainability, but they are also crucial to attempts to improve the social environment and make further improvements in human wellbeing.

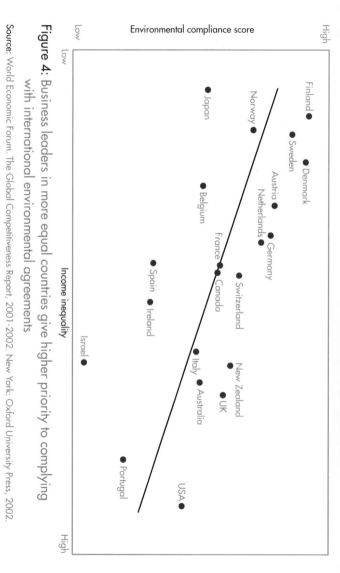

Figure 4: Business leaders in more equal countries give higher priority to complying with international environmental agreements

Source: World Economic Forum. The Global Competitiveness Report, 2001-2002. New York: Oxford University Press, 2002.

Equality and the Path to Environmental Sustainability

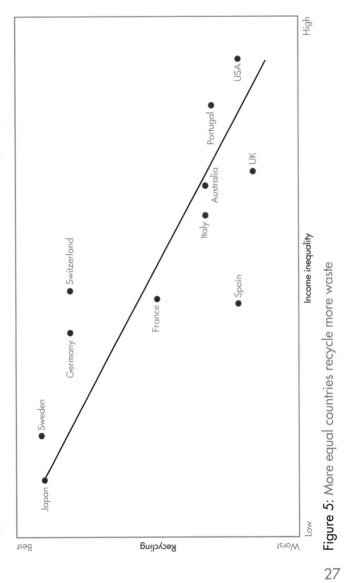

Figure 5: More equal countries recycle more waste

The rest of this pamphlet explores how we can make changes which will, in themselves, not only improve the quality of life and ease the transition to sustainability, but will also bring the additional benefits of reduced inequality.

3: A COUNTERVAILING FORCE

The ratio of the incomes of the top to the bottom 20 per cent of the population in the UK is around twice as high as it is in the more egalitarian of the rich developed market economies – including most of the Scandinavian countries. Before discussing policies which might reduce income differences, we should look briefly at what has driven the main changes in income distribution in the past.

Figure 6 shows the long-term trends in income inequality in various developed countries during most of the 20th century. The broad pattern shown there is much the same across the developed world. Inequality was high until the 1930s when a long decline in inequality starts. The timing of the start of the decline varies by 5–10 years from country to country and from one measure of income inequality to another. Inequality continues to decrease until sometime in the 1970s. But from around 1980, or a little later in some countries, inequality starts to grow again until, by the early 21st century, some countries have returned to levels of inequality not seen since the 1920s.

This pattern reflects first the strengthening, and then the weakening, of the labour movement during the 20th century. If you take the proportion of the labour force in trade unions as a measure of the strength of the labour movement's power as a

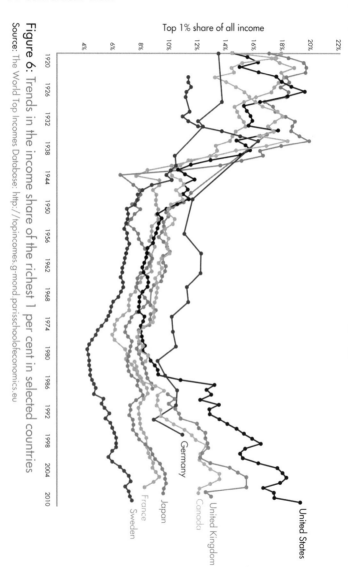

Figure 6: Trends in the income share of the richest 1 per cent in selected countries

Source: The World Top Incomes Database: http://topincomes.g-mond.parisschoolofeconomics.eu

countervailing voice and force in society, the relationship with inequality is very clear. Figure 7 shows the relation between inequality and the proportion of the labour force in trade unions in 16 OECD countries at various points btween 1966 and 1994.[39]

As trade union membership declined (to the left), inequality increased. Data on trade union membership for single countries over time during the 20th century confirms this relationship. As an example, Figure 8 shows that inequality declined in the USA as trade union strength increased and rose when trade union strength declined.[40]

However, the connection between trade union membership and inequality should not be seen as if it were simply a reflection of what trade unions do for the wages of their members. Instead the relationship indicates the strengthening and then the weakening of the ideological, political and industrial influence in society of progressive politics as a whole. What mattered was its strength as a countervailing voice in society. Accompanying that was of course also the fear of communism: when introducing the New Deal during the 1930s depression, President Roosevelt said it was necessary to "reform in order to preserve" the system. Although up to the end of the 1960s, communist central planning was often thought to be – despite its other faults – more efficient, with faster economic growth rates (even according to CIA estimates), that view was completely reversed during 1970s and 1980s.

The rise in inequality since around 1980 is largely attributable to the political power of the neoliberal ideology which came in with Reagan and Thatcher. Legislation was passed to weaken trade union power, utilities were privatised and top tax rates dramatically reduced. One of the effects of halving top tax rates from above 80 per cent was paradoxical. You might expect that if the rich were left with so much more after tax, that this would moderate their efforts to increase their salaries before tax. But instead of moderating the growth of

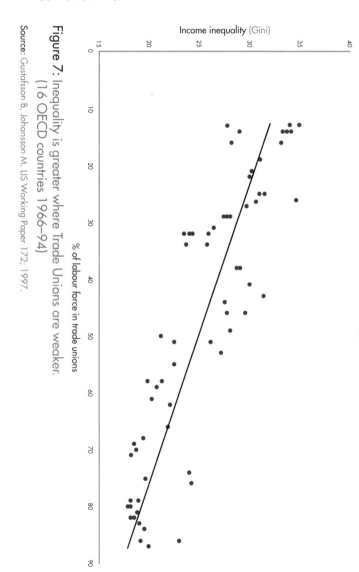

Figure 7: Inequality is greater where Trade Unions are weaker.
(16 OECD countries 1966-94)

Source: Gustafsson B., Johansson M. LIS Working Paper 172; 1997.

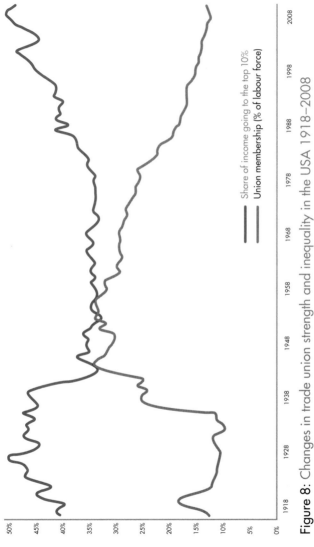

Figure 8: Changes in trade union strength and inequality in the USA 1918–2008

Source: Eisenbrey, R and Gordon, C. Economic Snapshot—unions and labor standards (2012).

Share of income going to the top 10%
Union membership (% of labour force)

pre-tax incomes at the top, it had the opposite effect: because the rich were allowed to keep a higher proportion of any income increase, it meant that additions to their pre-tax incomes were suddenly much more desirable as less would be lost in tax. As a result, there is a strong tendency across OECD countries for bigger reductions in top tax rates to be associated with *faster* increases in *pre-tax* incomes among the rich.[41] Not only that, but reductions in top tax rates are associated with lower economic growth rates.[42]

The role of politics – as opposed to strictly market forces – in the 20th century reduction and subsequent widening of inequality is also confirmed by a World Bank report on the eight countries (Japan, Republic of Korea, Taiwan, Singapore, Hong Kong, Thailand, Malaysia, Indonesia) which used to be known as the 'tiger economies'.[43] It described how, with well-publicised programs of 'shared growth', they all reduced their income differentials during the period 1960-1980. Policies variously included land reform, subsidies to lower fertilizer prices to boost rural incomes, wealth sharing programs, large scale public housing programs, and assistance to workers cooperatives. The World Bank report says that in each case, governments reduced inequality primarily because they faced challenges to their legitimacy, often from communist rivals, and needed to win wider popular support. For example, South Korea faced North Korea, Taiwan and Hong Kong faced the claims of China, and communist guerrilla forces operated widely. So here, as in the rich developed countries, it is a mistake to think that the main changes in inequality are simply the result of impersonal market forces rather than the outcome of political and ideological processes.[44]

The political pendulum

After moving to the right since the late 1970s, public opinion on inequality has begun to shift in a more progressive direction during the last few years. No doubt initiated by the financial crash of 2008 and spurred on by the Occupy movement, it has now been taken up by world leaders. President Obama called inequality "the defining challenge of our time". The Pope said it was "the root of social ills". The UN Secretary General, Ban Ki-Moon and the Director of the International Monetary Fund, Christine Lagarde, have made equally strong statements. Opinion polls in most countries show a very large majority of the population – sometimes as high as 80 per cent – think that income differences are too large, even though they underestimate how large they actually are.

As a result of this shift in opinion, there have been signs of some remedial action. The living wage movement has led many large public and private sector institutions to raise minimum pay rates for their staff.[45] In Britain, 16 or so local authorities controlled by the Labour party have set up Fairness Commissions to recommend policies for reducing income differences locally.[46] At the international level, the OECD has also taken action on tax avoidance by getting agreement from tax havens to share information on bank accounts with tax authorities.[47] However, in the six years since the financial crash there has so far been no general tendency for income differences in OECD countries to narrow.

It is clear that to win major reductions in inequality – for instance to bring inequality levels in OECD countries down even to the level of those which are currently least unequal – will require an enduring political movement with widespread public support. But although it is clear that inequality can be reduced by political pressure, it is also equally clear that as soon as that pressure weakens, the former inequalities quickly reassert themselves – as Figure 6 shows. As the left lost ground as a political force, much of the social progress it achieved during the 20th century has been undone.

The consequences of putting progress towards greater equality into reverse are unmistakable. Newspapers report that more households now employ domestic help or servants than at any time since the 19th century.[48,49]And while the bonus culture has established new dynasties in which inherited wealth will ensure a privileged few will never have to work, we see the re-emergence of soup kitchens in the form of 'food banks'.

There is one overwhelmingly important message to be learned from these reversals. What the left failed to do when it was at its peak in the late 1960s and early 1970s, was to make the structural changes which would prevent us going back to where we started. After swinging to the right for so long, the political pendulum has now changed direction and the possibility of achieving real progressive change may return. This time we need to be clear about the kind of structural changes which are needed to ensure that progress towards greater equality becomes permanent rather than being so easily reversed.

Structural change

If greater equality were to depend primarily on the redistribution of income, with pre-tax income differences undiminished, it would remain vulnerable. Redistribution through taxes and social security benefits can be undone at the stroke of any new government's pen. And it is particularly vulnerable when so many people regard taxes almost as a kind of legalised theft of incomes they feel they earned and have a right to.

The main source of widening income differences over the last few decades has been the tendency for top incomes

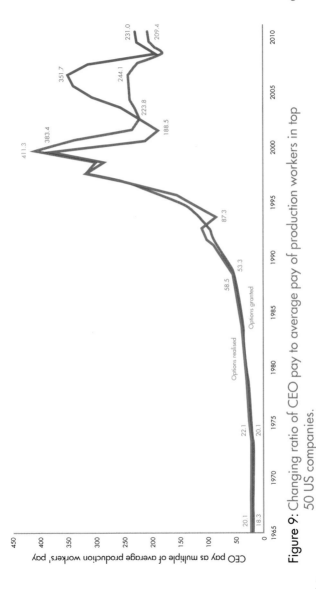

Figure 9: Changing ratio of CEO pay to average pay of production workers in top 50 US companies.

Source: Source: Mishel L, Sabadish N. Economic Policy Institute Brief #331. Washington, 2012 (before taxes) to increase much more rapidly than everyone else's. Figure 9 shows the widening of income differences in the biggest 350 American companies. Differentials between the CEOs of those companies and production workers averaged around 20:1 or 30:1 in the 1970s. By the first decade of this century these differentials had increased tenfold to between 200:1 and 400:1.[50]

These huge differentials are almost wholly confined to the private sector where they seem almost entirely unrelated to company performance.[51] In the public sector, whether in local government, health services, universities, the police and army, differentials are very much smaller – typically no more than 20:1 and sometimes as low as 10:1. The difference between the public and private sectors was also shown when CEO pay was dramatically increased in companies which were privatised during the 1980s.

The 'bonus culture' and the rapid rise of top incomes reflect a lack of any effective democratic constraint on the self-interest of the powerful – a lack of constraint whether exercised through taxes, trade unions or the rest of the labour movement. Our response should be to build effective democratic constraints permanently into the economic system. We need to develop policies to extend democracy into the economic sphere in ways which are consistent with, but modify the effects of, the market. Already about half the member countries of the European Union have some kind of legislative provision for employee representation on company boards or remuneration committees.[52, 53] A 2013 survey carried out in the UK (where there is no requirement for employee representation) found that 76 per cent of the population were in favour of employee representation on company boards.[54] Employee surveys in the USA also show that a large majority want more participation in decision making.[55] In Germany, different levels of employee representation are required for different sized companies. In companies with over 2000 employees, half the members of remuneration committees have to be employee representatives. Though the legislation differs in strength from country to country, and is often too weak to make much difference, studies suggest that companies which have employee representatives on their boards tend to have smaller income differences within them.[56] It also looks as if countries with stronger legislation of this kind have had smaller rises in inequality than countries without such legislation.

As well as stronger legislative provision for employee representation on company boards, we also need policies to develop the sector made up of more thorough-going democratic models such as employee co-operatives and employee-owned companies. More democratic models such as these have many advantages. First, income differences in co-operatives tend to be very much smaller than elsewhere. In the Mondragon group of co-operatives in Spain, employing around 80,000 people, top to bottom pay differences are often around 5:1 and rarely more than 9:1 – though there is a tendency for senior staff to be poached by other corporations. As well as reducing income differences, co-operatives and employee-owned companies also lead to a redistribution of wealth from external shareholders to employees and, simultaneously, reduce unearned income. It is also clear that they change working relationships and so improve the experience of work: as Robert Oakeshott says in his book *Jobs and Fairness*, an employee buyout can change a company from a piece of property into a community.[57] Although in many residential areas people have lost a sense of community, it is at work that we now have most to do with each other and ought to be able to rebuild a sense of community. We don't, because it is also at work that income differences are first created and we are most divided by hierarchical systems of 'line management'. Both by changing relationships at work and by reducing the scale of divisive income differences in society, more democratic economic institutions such as employee-owned companies and co-operatives, can help develop social cohesion and reciprocity at work, and strengthen community life more widely.[58, 59]

A crucial advantage of more democratic and egalitarian models of business is that they tend to have higher productivity. There have been numerous studies over many years which show not only that co-operatives and employee-owned business tend to have economic advantages but that even gestures towards 'participative management' and profit sharing bring reliable improvements in productivity.[60, 61, 62, 63, 64] The evidence on this point is pretty robust.

But perhaps the most important reason to develop the co-operative and employee-owned business sector is the connection between greater equality and sustainability. It was Murray Bookchin, an American pioneer of the environmental movement, who said that corporations "can no more be 'persuaded' to limit growth than a human being can be 'persuaded' to stop breathing." This focus on growth comes both from the need to maximise returns to external shareholders and from the way businesses work as systems for concentrating wealth and power at the top. Despite occasional recognition of the need to rethink, there is, in the absence of structural change, little sign that the power of the profit motive and of the self-aggrandisement of many of those at the top, is self-limiting.[65]

Co-operatives on the other hand are more likely to act as communities and not to want to expand at any price. For the same reasons, they also seem more likely to perform well in ethical and environmental terms. A study of employees in 22 companies with contrasting levels of organisational democracy, in Austria, Italy and Germany, concluded that greater democracy not only improves the 'socio-moral' climate within the company, but also increases employees 'civic virtues', 'pro-social perspective-taking' and mutual aid.[66, 67] But to ensure that more democratically constituted companies act in the public interest, there is no reason why their boards should not include representatives of the community and consumers along with employee representatives.

4: SPREADING ECONOMIC DEMOCRACY

Most companies make little or no gesture towards employee democracy, despite the very large majority of employees who want systems which give them more participation and voice in decision making.[68, 69] As a result, employees are more likely to feel a sense of disaffection, partly because they know that they are being used to serve the interests of others (external shareholders or those in receipt of profits), and partly because of the petty annoyances often caused by institutional systems set up to ensure that they do.

These issues are far from trivial. Whether or not people have a sense of control over their work has been found to exert, through chronic stress, a major influence on health.[70] And maximising people's control over their work in the context of modern production implies the need for greater workplace democracy.[71] But broader issues of institutional injustice, and whether people feel they are fairly treated, have also been found to damage health – including accelerating the speed at which mental functioning declines with age.[72, 73, 74] Because feeling treated unfairly is such a powerful stressor, the effects are not confined to the work place: a study covering school children in 21 countries found that in 19 of them children suffered more headaches when they felt unfairly treated by their teacher.[75]

The evidence that job changing is consistently lower in more democratic companies suggests that people prefer working in them. This is also supported by the fact that they are usually overrepresented in lists of the best employers to work for. The frequent – often unspoken – animosity and friction which many employees feel towards their bosses is likely to be less common in co-ops and employee-owned companies – particularly so where senior managers are accountable to employees who may also have a direct or indirect role in their appointment.

Another reason for supporting all types of economic democracy is that the existing forms of company ownership and control are becoming a counter-productive anachronism. A report from the British TUC called *Workers on Board*, describes how the traditional form of share ownership has become an increasingly inappropriate system for owning and controlling business.[76] It points out how in the 1960s most shares were owned by individuals with a longer-term interest in a small number of companies which they often had some knowledge of. People owned shares in the same company for an average of seven years. But now, in many countries, the vast majority of shares are owned by financial institutions which spread their investments across hundreds or even thousands of companies. Because they make money through short-term share trading, often triggered by computer algorithms, the average length of time they own a share is thought to be less than a minute, hence they have no long-term interest or knowledge of these companies. Even outside these high frequency trading systems, shares are on average owned for only a few months. The TUC report says that this has reached a point where a large listed company may have thousands or even tens of thousands of shareholders and find it difficult even to get full information on who its share owners are.

At the same time, modern production increasingly involves the integration of the expertise and knowledge of many different people, so much so that the value of a company is now less a matter of its buildings and capital equipment than of the value of the group of employees with their integrated skills, specialised knowledge and know-how. This means that buying and selling a company amounts to buying and selling a group of people – an appallingly anachronistic process, especially when that group of people could be running their own company democratically.

But if companies with more democratic structures tend to have higher productivity, and modern shareholding has become so anachronistic, why don't we see rapid extensions of democracy into the economic sphere? The answer is that companies do not exist simply to produce the goods and services that we all need. They also serve to concentrate enormous power and wealth in the hands of a few people at the top – and that is a function we don't need. It means that the so-called 'captains of industry', face a huge conflict of interests and may not have the welfare of their companies at heart.

The turnover of many national corporations is larger than the GDP of many whole countries. A few are larger even than countries like Norway and New Zealand, and yet they are free to exercise that extraordinary concentration of undemocratic power and wealth as they please. They run rings round national governments, and often pay little or no tax. In 2008 the US Government Accountability Office reported that 83 of the USA's biggest 100 corporations used subsidiaries in tax havens to avoid tax. The Tax Justice Network said that 99 of the 100 biggest companies in Europe did the same. And yet they depend on the entire publicly funded infrastructure – from transport systems to education and the police – which others pay for.

Large corporations play an increasingly antisocial role in society. Freudenberg in his book *Lethal but Legal* provides copious and detailed evidence that the food, tobacco, alcohol, gun, pharmaceutical, agribusiness and automobile industries are now among the most significant threats to public health. In the endless conflicts between public and corporate interests, they of course defend themselves to the hilt. They use their huge advertising wealth, media and political influence, to counter evidence of risk coming from scientific research and to fight any legislative attempts to reduce risk. They pack regulatory systems with people who will defend their interests, they spend huge amounts on lobbying politicians, and continue to sell their products in the face of massive evidence of harm – from excessive obesity, drunkenness, shootings, environmental damage, and so on. And on top of it all, the whole business effort, with its sophisticated marketing and advertising, still aims to maximise sales and consumerism even when we know carbon emissions have to be reduced by at least 80 per cent to save us from the worst effects of global warming. It should not be beyond the wit of modern societies to ensure that production is undertaken in the service of the public good, humanity and the planet. The obstacle is that large corporations are so powerful that our democratically elected politicians are afraid to touch them, and that means far too afraid to start thinking about alternatives.

The policy implications

Rather than incurring costs, reducing inequality leads to major savings. The Equality Trust calculated that the high level of inequality in the UK costs £39bn a year. That is the estimated saving just from improvements in physical and mental health, reductions in violence and in imprisonment, to be gained by reducing income differences in the UK just to the average levels of inequality in OECD countries. In terms of the total human costs the benefits of greater equality are incalculable.

In the 1970s, Britain was as equal as the Scandinavian countries are now. But since then the gap between the richest and poorest 20 per cent in Britain has widened so rapidly that it is now twice as big as in Scandinavia. Much the greater part of that widening happened in the 1980s under Thatcher. Although international comparisons show that it is clearly beneficial to health and wellbeing to halve our inequality, we do not have the data to tell us how much further than that it would be beneficial to go. However, halving the income gap between the top and bottom 20 per cent, or to get back to the levels of inequality which existed in the 1970s, will not be achieved overnight. It will require a sustained political movement with this as its main objective. By the time we've regained that level of inequality there may be data which can tell us how much further we should go.

The role of top incomes in increasing inequality matters just as much as poverty and low incomes. Equality can be increased by reducing income differences either before tax or by redistributing incomes through progressive taxes and more generous benefits. Judging from examples of more equal countries or American states, how a society becomes more equal is less important than how equal it becomes. Both approaches seem to bring the social benefits of greater equality. But an important difference between reducing income differences before or after taxes is that any progress towards more progressive taxation can more easily be reversed by an incoming government than can increases in economic democracy. Increases in economic democracy ensure that greater equality is more deep-seated in the fabric of society.

As we highlighted earlier, action to tackle offshore tax havens has already begun and is clearly a necessary preliminary to making taxes much more progressive again. A number of countries have also seen moves to increase minimum wages or to get employers to pay a 'living wage' substantially above the minimum.

Because greater equality seems to diminish prejudice against those lower on the social ladder, greater equality might also make it easier to provide a more generous system of benefits. If greater economic democracy also made employment more congenial, there might be less worry that more generous benefits would make people workshy.

A key to reducing income differences before tax is for government management of the economy to maintain low unemployment and a tight labour market so that there is competition for labour. Historically, as figures 7 and 8 show, trade unions have also played a key role in reducing inequality. Their ability to represent and act on behalf of their members needs to be restored.

To help maintain an orderly wage bargaining system and to counter low incomes among the non-unionised, we also need to re-establish the wages councils to set national wages agreements in different sectors of the economy.

More fundamental proposals to reform taxes and benefit systems include plans for a basic income and for a land tax. Both are widely discussed and advocated by academics and policy experts and have a lot to recommend them.[77,78,79]

However, the long-term goal must be to reduce pre-tax income differences by extending democracy into the economic sphere. While there will of course be resistance to such policies, it is crucial to recognise that there is likely to be a divergence of interests between the personal interests of very highly paid company executives and what would be in the real benefit of their companies. This means that policy initiatives developed to extend economic democracy will often be opposed by ideological interpretations of economic realities which owe more to the desire of the rich to justify and protect their interests than to serve the greater good. This is an important point because policy development will require a great deal of discussion which the self-serving ideology of the rich will constantly threaten to derail. In the past, the political interests of the less well-off were partly protected by the view that different class interests gave rise to different class ideologies. But when political leaders of even progressive political parties get too close to the wealthy and aspire to join them, rival ideologies are soon eclipsed.

The democratisation of the economy needs to be a publicly recognised political objective. Opposition will be strong: extensions to democracy are rarely supported by those whose power they would curtail. The objective should be advocated and defended by all progressive politicians as the next major step in human emancipation. We need to create a popular understanding that this is part of a transition to a sustainable future capable of achieving a higher quality of life than is possible now. Rather than being a revolution, it is a gradual but vital transformation.

To help in this process, the profile of the 490 employee-owned and co-operative businesses in the UK needs to be raised. According to Co-operatives UK, they have a combined annual turnover of £10.7bn and employ close to 100,000 people. Attention also needs to be drawn to the other highly successful, progressive, business models as exemplified by large companies like Arup, Scott Bader, Tullis Russell, Swann-Morton and John Lewis. And of course the same applies to the many successful examples in other countries.

A first step would be to set up an internet portal which allowed people to do their shopping from democratic businesses. It would also be helpful to set up a 'democratic company' logo, perhaps modelled on the 'fair trade' example, to increase the visibility of these companies. As well as giving the more democratic sector of the economy an additional market advantage, it would also increase public awareness of the practical and ethical superiority of more democratic business models. At its simplest, such a website could provide users with links to companies with more democratic business models which sold the categories of goods you were looking for. But with more development, it could work more like a version of Amazon (but paying its taxes and treating employees fairly). As well as being restricted to more democratic companies, it might also exclude any of those companies which had unacceptably large pay differentials.

While raising the expansion of economic democracy in the public mind and placing it at the centre of the political agenda, the first policy objective should be to require, by law, that all but the smallest companies should have employee representatives on company boards and remuneration committees. The proportion of employees on these bodies should be higher in companies with larger numbers of employees. We suggest that the smallest companies should be exempt because it is predominantly the larger companies that create the possibility for more layers in the social hierarchy, bigger social distances and wider pay differentials.

As part of communicating the long-term intention of democratising the economy, the proportions of employee representatives on company boards and remuneration committees could be set to increase over time, moving eventually to majority control and beyond. Another way of setting up a gradual transfer of power might be to include a requirement that a small proportion of shares should be transferred each year to employee-controlled trusts. If just two per cent were transferred each year, employees would be in majority control after 25 years. Perhaps before making either of these a legal requirement, conformity with conditions such as these could be made a condition of gaining public sector contracts or lower corporation tax rates.

In Rhode Island and California, there have already been legislative initiatives to reduce corporation taxes for companies with smaller pay ratios and to give them preferential treatment when awarding government contracts. Elsewhere there are initiatives to use public expenditure to support the development of a co-operative and sustainable local economy. One is the Democracy Collaborative which started in Cleveland, Ohio. It funnels the expenditure of local public sector 'anchor' institutions – such as the local university and city government – towards co-operatives and 'community wealth building' initiatives and has led to the establishment of the 'Evergreen Co-operative' based on the Mondragon model, the hugely successful Spanish co-operative group. Preston in Lancashire has begun a similar initiative with agreement from local public sector institutions willing to divert a higher proportion of their expenditure to support local wealth building.

The Employee Ownership Association and Co-operatives UK have detailed policy proposals which would accelerate the growth of co-operatives and employee ownership. Both organisations suggest that a major obstacle to the development of this sector is the lack of knowledge of these models among professional legal and financial advisers. This means more democratic models are not suggested as an option at key stages in business development – for instance when business are started, when they plan major expansions, have to deal with succession or rescue issues. The lack of awareness among the professions would of course be diminished if we succeeded in increasing the public awareness more generally as discussed earlier. But it is also suggested that the Department for Business, Innovation and Skills should promote a single route to employee ownership and establish the necessary legislative support. The department should also provide a training and advice service on how to set up employee owned and co-operative companies.

There are also frequent difficulties in arranging bank loans to help fund employee buyouts. Arrangements should be made to ensure funds are more easily available. But ideally, a government should work out a complete package of measures to grow the democratic sector, complete with tax incentives, sources of advice and support, readymade rules of governance and sources of finance.

The constitutions of employee-owned and co-operative business should in all cases be designed to prevent employees selling their companies back to external shareholders. The absence of effective provisions of this kind has in the past led to major waves of 'demutualisation' and prevented a faster growth of the more democratic sector.

Lastly, employees taking on new functions on company boards would need a variety of options for training in areas such as management, business law, accountancy and economics. Options should range from some of the learning schemes designed to prepare school governors, to the provision of master's degrees to which people could be seconded. As well as improving the confidence of elected board members and the quality of their decision making, the provision of preparatory courses would also communicate the seriousness of a government's commitment to seeing this transition through.

To decide that it is unrealistic to plan changes as sweeping as we have described here means accepting that we will be defeated by climate change. The political failure to produce adequate responses to what climate change means for our societies and for humanity shows an appalling lack of leadership and responsibility in the face of overwhelming evidence. And there is no doubt whatsoever that the longer we delay, the more sudden, difficult and traumatic, the transition to low carbon economies will have to be.

CONCLUSION

We have put greater equality at the centre of the strategy for creating a better society because it goes to the heart of social relations in society at large. Social status systems among humans (like dominance ranking systems or pecking orders among animals) are orderings based on power and status which ensure privileged access to resources for those at the top, regardless of the needs of others. The fact that humans, like members of any other species, all have the same basic needs as each other, means that there is always the question of whether to share access to scarce resources or compete as rivals. Do we live in a society based on co-operation and reciprocity, or competition and rivalry?

Hobbes was close to the truth when he put the question of how to avoid conflict – the threat of "warre of each against all" – at the centre of his politics. But the answer goes much deeper than the need for a sovereign government capable of keeping the peace. People share food and eat together socially because that enshrines the overriding importance of not competing for access to basic necessities. The same message is of course repeated in the religious symbolism of the communion. Even words like 'companion' ('Compañero' in Spanish and 'Copain' in French) come from the Latin 'con' (with) and 'pan' (bread) and means that your friends are people with whom you share food. Similarly, gifts are a symbol of friendship because they show in the most concrete terms that giver and receiver recognise each other's needs. And in some societies to refuse a gift is tantamount to a declaration of war.

In effect, we have – deep within our psyche – two fundamentally different social strategies, one to do with friendship and the other to do with superiority and inferiority. We all know how to make and value friends and we all know how snobbishness, downward prejudice and social climbing work. How much we use each of these strategies has repercussions throughout the rest of social life; it colours our psychology and social customs.

What Hobbes did not know but which we now do, is that in the societies of human prehistory, before the development of government, people kept the peace by putting gift exchange, food sharing and a high degree of equality at the foundation of their social systems. And they did that, as the American anthropologist Marshal Sahlins has pointed out, to avoid the conflict which comes from competition for access to scarce resources.[82] It is now clear, from records covering some 200 hunting and gathering societies, that for more than 90 per cent of human existence, we typically lived in societies with an extraordinary degree of equality.[81, 82]

Human beings have an inherited sensitivity to hierarchy. Because material differences give rise to social distances, to feelings of superiority and inferiority, the degree of social hierarchy and the importance of status ranking serve as indicators of how far a society departs from egalitarian systems. And the further it departs from mutuality, reciprocity and sharing, the stronger the message that we will have to fend for ourselves. That is why when inequality increases, societies become more antisocial, people become more worried about status, community life weakens, we trust each other less, we pay less attention to the common good, violence increases and we are less willing to help each other.

At the heart of progressive politics there has always been an intuition that inequality is divisive and socially corrosive. What has changed is that we now have the internationally comparable data which proves that intuition is true. What it means is that if we want to create a classless society, we must start by reducing the material inequalities between us.

It should be clear from what has already been said that we are only likely to be able to achieve the fundamental trans-formation of our economy and way of life if we also make equally fundamental social changes. We need to reduce the extraordinarily wasteful status competition which drives conspicuous consumption. We also need to increase our willingness to act for the common good. The good news is that making these changes opens the way to very substantial improvements in wellbeing for the vast majority of the popu-lation. Moving towards sustainability involves opening up a new era of improvements in the quality of life – no longer the diminishing returns from growth, but real gains from what greater equality does for social relationships and the quality of the social environment.

The transition to sustainability is therefore a transition to a society which is better for all of us. There are four major improvements in the quality of life which are necessary to prepare the ground for sustainability.

First, through greater equality, we gain a world where status matters less, where the awkward divisions of class begin to heal, where social anxieties are less inhibiting of social interaction and people are less plagued by issues of confidence and low self-esteem. The result is that we feel less need for the drink and drugs we (particularly young people) use to cope with anxiety and to ease social contact, less need for narcissistic self-presentation, less need to overspend for the sake of appearances. In short, we move towards a more relaxed social life in which it is easier to enjoy the pleasures of friendship and conviviality and gain a society better able to meet our basic social needs.

Second, we move from a society which maximises consumption to a society that uses each increase in productivity to gain more leisure and reduce the demands of work. We need more time for family and for our children, more time to care for each other, for friends, for the elderly and to enjoy community life. The New Economics Foundation has suggested that we should aim for a 21 hour week. Large international differences in working hours seem not to affect GNP per head.[85]

In future, annual increases in productivity must be turned into annual reductions in working hours. With a typical long-term increase in labour productivity of 2 per cent a year, in ten years' time we could all enjoy the same material standard of living but have an extra day off a week. But with more workplace democracy and shorter hours, the productivity growth rate might rise to 3 per cent a year. That would give us an extra day off a week within 7 years and the working week would be halved within 24 years. If, as some studies suggest, almost half of all jobs may be vulnerable to computerisation and automation,[84] cutting hours and sharing work will become increasingly important if we are to enjoy the benefits of technical progress.

Third is the improvement in the quality of working life resulting from the extension of democracy into employment. The current anachronistic system in which the control of companies – groups of people – can be bought and sold must be phased out. The purpose of much of what still remains the normal rigid inhuman ranking system, with line management and institutionalised hierarchy, is to exclude people from control over their work and ensure that it serves the interests of others. Working in democratic institutions such as co-operatives and employee-owned businesses (with or without community and consumer representatives), management becomes answerable to employees. Hierarchy becomes overlaid with social obligations and status divisions are reduced by very much smaller income differences. The next great stage in human emancipation must therefore be the extension of democracy into working life. Work should be where we get a sense of self-worth and of making a valued contribution. We can no longer accept a system of employment which reduces the lives of so many to a demeaned shadow of their potential.

Fourth come all the health and social benefits of living in a more equal society – the pattern we showed in *The Spirit Level* which reflects a body of evidence from research workers round the world which has been accumulating over the last 35 years. More equal societies bring major reductions in almost all the problems that become more common lower down the social ladder. A more equal society would enjoy better physical and mental health, higher standards of child wellbeing, less violence, fewer people in prison, less drug addiction and more equal opportunities for children. A more equal society is more conducive to the psychosocial wellbeing of the whole population.

As well as making very major improvements in the quality of our lives, these improvements in the social functioning of our societies will put environmental sustainability within our reach.

Change on such a scale can only be achieved if large numbers of people commit themselves to achieving it. Sometime after the late 1970s the political left lost its conviction that a better form of society was possible and left the way open for the rise of neoliberalism.

But now, facing the evidence of global warming and very dangerous climate change, the world has never been in greater need of a radical alternative. It is now urgent that progressive forces in society should clarify an inspiring view of a future society which is not only environmentally sustainable, but in which the real quality of life is better for the vast majority. Only then will people commit themselves to the long task of bringing that society into being.

Far from idealism, this is a necessary response to the likely damage and dislocation which climate change holds in store for us. And if we are to find the will to make the necessary changes, it is essential that we do so by creating a better and more attractive society able to satisfy human needs and raise the real quality of our lives. To try instead to hold down the unaddressed pressures of consumerism, profit maximisation and status seeking, is doomed to failure. Present structures are, after all, not a very efficient way of producing human wellbeing.

A major advantage of having a shared conception of a better society is that it gives a coherence to policy. Instead of the small steps which governments are able to take appearing as a rag-bag of uncoordinated policies, they start to be seen as steps in a consistent direction. But a vision of a better future can also reinvigorate some of the idealism and principle which so often seems to have become submerged in a politics driven by opportunism and expediency.

Endnotes

(Most of the references are freely available on Google Scholar)

1. Cutler D, Deaton A, Lleras-Muney A. The Determinants of Mortality. *Journal of Economic Perspectives* 2006;20(3):97-120.

2. Hansen J, Sato M, Kharecha P, Beerling D, Berner R, Masson-Delmotte V, et al. Target Atmospheric CO_2: Where Should Humanity Aim? *Open Atmospheric Science Journal* 2008;2:217-31.

3. Rahmstorf S. Modeling sea level rise. *Nature Education Knowledge* 2012;3(10):4.

4. Parry M, Palutikof J, Hanson C, Lowe J. Squaring up to reality. Nature Reports Climate Change 2008;2:68-70.

5. Economics, reality and the myths of growth. Osterreichishes Institut fur Wirtschaftsforschung; 2013; Vienna.

6. Jolly A. *Lucy's legacy: sex and intelligence in human evolution:* Harvard University Press, 2001.

7. Clark AE, Frijters P, Shields MA. Relative income, happiness, and utility: An explanation for the Easterlin paradox and other puzzles. *Journal of Economic Literature* 2008:95-144.

8. Easterlin RA, McVey LA, Switek M, Sawangfa O, Zweig JS. The happiness–income paradox revisited. *Proceedings of the National Academy of Sciences* 2010;107(52):22463-68

9. Easterlin RA. Happiness and Economic Growth: The Evidence. Discussion Paper. Bonn: IZA, Institute for the Study of Labor, 2013.

10. Wilkinson RG, Pickett KE. 2009. *The spirit level: why more equal societies almost always do better*, London, Penguin.

11. Wilkinson RG, Pickett KE. 2014. The Robb Lectures (I-III): The Human Cost of Inequality. University of Auckland. https://www.auckland.ac.nz/en/about/perspectives/public-lectures/robb-lectures-2014-professors-kate-pickett-and-richard-wilkins.html

12. Pickett KE, Wilkinson RG. Forthcoming. Income inequality and health: A causal review. Bethesda, MD: US NIH and the Agency for Healthcare Research & Quality (AHRQ).

13. Pickett KE, Wilkinson RG. Forthcoming. The ethical and policy implications of research on income inequality and child wellbeing. *Pediatrics*.

14. Subramanian SV, Kawachi I. Whose health is affected by income inequality? A multilevel interaction analysis of contemporaneous and lagged effects of state income inequality on individual self-rated health in the United States. *Health Place* 2006;12(2):141-56.

15. Layte, R. & Whelan, C. T. Who Feels Inferior? A Test of the Status Anxiety Hypothesis of Social Inequalities in Health. *European Sociological Review*, jcu057 (2014).

16. Messias E, Eaton WW, Grooms AN. Economic grand rounds: Income inequality and depression prevalence across the United States: an ecological study. *Psychiatr Serv* 2011;62(7):710-2.

17. Pickett KE, Wilkinson RG. Inequality: an underacknowledged source of mental illness and distress. *British Journal of Psychiatry* 2010;197:426-8.

18. Burns JK, Tomita A, Kapadia AS. Income inequality and schizophrenia: Increased schizophrenia incidence in countries with high levels of income inequality. *International Journal of Social Psychiatry* 2013.

19. Twenge JM, Konrath S, Foster JD, Campbell WK, Bushman BJ. Egos inflating over time: a cross-temporal meta-analysis of the Narcissistic Personality Inventory. *Journal of Personality*, 2008;76(4):875-902; discussion 03-28.

20. Loughnan S, Kuppens P, Allik J, Balazs K, de Lemus S, Dumont K, et al. Economic inequality is linked to biased self-perception. *Psychological science* 2011;22(10):1254-8.

21. Dickerson SS, Kemeny ME. Acute stressors and cortisol responses: a theoretical integration and synthesis of laboratory research. *Psychological Science*, 2004;130(3):355-91.

22. Wilkinson R G, Pickett KE. Income inequality and population health: A review and explanation of the evidence. Social Science & Medicine 62, 1768-1784 (2006).

23. Holt-Lunstad J, Smith TB, Layton JB. Social relationships and mortality risk: a meta-analytic review. *PLoS Med* 2010;7(7):e1000316.

24. Cohen S, Doyle WJ, Skoner DP, Rabin BS, Gwaltney JM, Jr. Social ties and susceptibility to the common cold. *Journal of the American Medical Association* 1997;277(24):1940-4.

25. Kiecolt-Glaser JK, Loving TJ, Stowell JR, Malarkey WB, Lemeshow S, Dickinson SL, et al. Hostile marital interactions, proinflammatory cytokine production, and wound healing. *Arch Gen Psychiatry* 2005;62(12):1377-84.

26. Helliwell JF, Putnam RD. The social context of well-being. *Philosophical transactions-royal society of London series B biological sciences* 2004:1435-46.

27. Myers DC. 1999. Close Relationships and Quality of Life. *Well-being: Foundations of Hedonic Psychology*, 374.

28. Pinquart M, Sörensen S. Influences of socioeconomic status, social network, and competence on subjective well-being in later life: a meta-analysis. *Psychology and Aging* 2000;15(2):187.

29. Layard R. *Happiness: Lessons from a New Science.* London: Allen Lane, 2005.

30. Bowles S, Park Y. Emulation, inequality, and work hours: was Thorsten Veblen right? *The Economic Journal* 2005;115:F397-F412.

31. Kumhof M, Rancière R. Inequality, Leverage and Crises. *Working Paper*: International Monetary Fund, 2010.

32. Adkisson RV, Saucedo E. Emulation and state-by-state variations in bankruptcy rates. *The Journal of Socio-Economics* 2012;41(4):400-07.

33. Johnson SL, Leedom LJ, Muhtadie L. 2012. The dominance behavioral system and psychopathology: evidence from self-report, observational, and biological studies. *Psychological Bulletin*, 138, 692-743.

34. Dittmar H, Bond R, Hurst M, Kasser T. A meta-analysis of the materialism literature. *Unpublished manuscript, University of Sussex, Brighton*, UK 2013.

35. Meltzer H, Bebbington P, Brugha T, Farrell M, Jenkins R. The relationship between personal debt and specific common mental disorders. *The European Journal of Public Health* 2012:cks021.

36. Paskov M, Dewilde C. Income inequality and solidarity in Europe. *Research in Social Stratification and Mobility* 2012.

37. World Economic Forum 2002. *The Global Competitiveness Report*, 2001. New York: Oxford University Press.

38. Motesharrei S, Rivas J, Kalnay E. Human and nature dynamics (HANDY): Modeling inequality and use of resources in the collapse or sustainability of societies. *Ecological Economics* 2014;101:90-102.

39. Gustafsson B, Johansson M. In search of smoking guns: What makes income inequality vary over time in different countries? *American Sociological Review* 1999:585-605.

40. Eisenbrey RG, C. As unions decline, inequality rises. http://www.epi.org/publication/unions-decline-inequality-rises/ Washington: Economic Policy Institute, 2012.

41. Piketty T, Saez E, Stantcheva S. Optimal taxation of top labor incomes: A tale of three elasticities: National Bureau of Economic Research, 2011.

42. Ostry MJD, Berg MA, Tsangarides MCG. *Redistribution, Inequality, and Growth:* International Monetary Fund, 2014.

43. World Bank. *The East Asian miracle.* Oxford: Oxford University Press, 1993.

44. Krugman P. *The conscience of a liberal:* WW Norton & Company, 2009.

45. Living Wage Commission. *Work that pays.* London, 2014.

46. Bunyan PD, J. Approaches to reducing poverty and inequality in the UK. *A Study of Civil Society Initiatives and Fairness Commissions.* Edge Hill, UK.: Webb Memorial Trust, 2014.

47. Houlder V. Switzerland pledges to lift veil on tax secrecy. *Financial Times* 2014 6 May 2014.

48. Mount H. Are you being served? *Daily Telegraph* 2013 28 April 2013.

49. Gibbons K. Extra home help gives Britain that Downton feeling. *The Times* 31st January 2014.

50. Mishel L, Sabadish N. Pay and the top 1%: How executive compensation and financial-sector pay have fuelled income inequality. Issue Brief: Economic Policy Institute, 2012.

51. Tosi HL, Werner S, Katz JP, Gomez-Mejia LR. How much does performance matter? A meta-analysis of CEO pay studies. *Journal of Management* 2000;26(2):301-39.

52. Schulten TZ, S. Board level employee representation in Europe. http://www.eurofound.europa.eu/eiro/1998/09/study/tn9809201s.htm: Eurofound, 1998.

53. Conchon AK, N. Stollt, M. Worker board-level participation in the 31 European Economic Area countries. http://www.worker-participation.eu/National-Industrial-Relations/Across-Europe/Board-level-Representation2/TABLE-Worker-board-level-participation-in-the-31-European-Economic-Area-countries: European Trade Union Institute, 2013.

54. Survation 2013. Employment Survey II. 6 February 2013 http://survation.com/wp-content/uploads/2014/04/Employment-II-Full-Tables.pdf: Survation.

55. Freeman RB, Rogers J. 2006. *What workers want.* Cornell University Press.

56. Vitols S. 2010. Board level employee representation, executive remuneration and firm performance in large European companies. European Corporate Governance Institute and European Trade Union Institute.

57. Oakeshott R. *Jobs and fairness: the logic and experience of employee ownership.* Norwich: Michael Russell, 2000.

58. Zeuli K. Radel J. 2005. Cooperatives as a community development strategy: linking theory and practice. *Journal of Regional Analysis and Policy,* 35, 43-54.

59. Azevedo A. Gitahy, L. 2010. The Cooperative Movement, Self-Management and Competitiveness: The case of Mondragon Corporacion Cooperativa. Working USA, 13, 5-29.

60. Estrin S, Jones DC, Svejnar J. The productivity effects of worker participation: Producer cooperatives in western economies. *Journal of Comparative Economics* 1987;11(1):40-61.

61. Jones DC. 1987. The productivity effects of worker directors and financial participation by employees in the firm: the case of British retail cooperatives. *Industrial and Labor Relations Review*, 79-92.

62. Fitzroy FR, Kraft K. 1987. Cooperation, productivity, and profit sharing. *The Quarterly Journal of Economics*, 23-35.

63. Becchetti L, Castriota S, Tortia EC. 2013. Productivity, wages and intrinsic motivations. *Small Business Economics*, 41, 379-399.

64. Blasi JR, Freeman RB, Kruse DL. 2013. *The Citizen's Share: Putting Ownership Back Into Democracy*, Yale University Press.

65. Kelly M. 2002. The next step for CSR: building economic democracy. *Business Ethics*, 16, 2-7.

66. Weber WG, Unterrainer C, Schmid BE. The influence of organizational democracy on employees' socio-moral climate and prosocial behavioral orientations. *Journal of Organizational Behavior* 2009;30(8):1127-49.

67. Verdorfer AP, Weber WG, Unterrainer C, Seyr S. 2013. The relationship between organizational democracy and socio-moral climate: Exploring effects of the ethical context in organizations. *Economic and Industrial Democracy*, 34, 423-449.

68. Freeman RB, Rogers J. *What workers want:* Cornell University Press, 2006.

69. Freeman RB, Boxall PF, Haynes P. 2007. *What workers say: Employee voice in the Anglo-American workplace*, Cornell University Press.

70. Bosma H, Marmot MG, Hemingway H, Nicholson AC, Brunner E, Stansfeld SA. Low job control and risk of coronary heart disease in Whitehall II (prospective cohort) study. *British Medical Journal* 1997;314(7080):558-65.

71. Theorell T. Democracy at work and its relationship to health. In: Perrewe P, Ganster DE, editors. *Emotional and physiological processes and intervention strategies*. Greenwich, CT: JAI Press, 2003.

72. De Vogli R, Brunner E, Marmot MG. 2007. Unfairness and the social gradient of metabolic syndrome in the Whitehall II Study. *Journal of Psychosomatic Research*, 63, 413-419.

73. De Vogli R, Ferrie JE, Chandola T, Kivimaki M, Marmot MG. 2007. Unfairness and health: evidence from the Whitehall II Study. *Journal of Epidemiology and Community Health*, 61, 513-518.

74. Elovainio M, Singh-Manoux A, Ferrie JE, Shipley M, Gimeno D, De Vogli R, Vahtera J, Virtanen M, Jokela M, Marmot MG. 2012. Organisational justice and cognitive function in middle-aged employees: the Whitehall II study. *Journal of Epidemiology and Community Health*, 66, 552-556.

75. Lenzi M, Vieno A, De Vogli R, Santinello M, Ottova V, Baška T, et al. Perceived teacher unfairness and headache in adolescence: a cross-national comparison. *International Journal of Public Health* 2013;58(2):227-35.

76. Williamson J. 2013. *Workers on Board: The case for workers' voice in corporate governance*. Trade Unions Congress, London.

77. Widerquist K, Sheahen A. The United States: The Basic Income Guarantee–Past Experience, Current Proposals. *Basic Income Worldwide: Horizons of Reform* 2012:11.

78. Gilroy BM, Heimann A, Schopf M. Basic Income and Labour Supply: The German Case. *Basic Income Studies* 2012;8(1):43-70.

79. Dye RF, England RW. *Assessing the theory and practice of land value taxation*: Lincoln Institute of Land Policy, 2010.

80. Sahlins M. *Stone age economics*. London: Routledge, 2003.

81. Boehm C. 2012. *Moral origins: The evolution of virtue, altruism, and shame*, Basic Books.

82. Erdal D, Whiten A. 1996. Egalitarianism and Machiavellian intelligence in human evolution In: Mellars P, Gibson K. (eds.) *Modelling the early human mind*. Cambridge: McDonald Institute Monographs.

83. Coote A, Franklin J, Simms A, Murphy M. 2010. *21 Hours: Why a Shorter Working Week Can Help Us All to Flourish in the 21st Century*, New Economics Foundation.

84. Frey BD, Osborne M. The future of employment: how susceptible are jobs to computerisation? 2013, University of Oxford.

Discussion Guide: A Convenient Truth

How to use this Discussion Guide
The guide can be used in various ways by
Fabian Local Societies, local political party
meetings and trade union branches, student
societies, NGOs and other groups.

- You might hold a discussion among local members or
  invite a guest speaker – for example, an MP, academic
  or local practitioner to lead a group discussion.

- Some different key themes are suggested. You might
  choose to spend 15–20 minutes on each area, or
  decide to focus the whole discussion on one of the
  issues for a more detailed discussion.

A discussion could address some or all of the following questions:

1. Wilkinson and Pickett accuse the left of being 'rudderless' and having given up on a vision of creating a better society for everyone. Has Labour lost its sense of vision? Does it need one or is 'utopian' politics not suitable for today's world?

2. The authors suggest that consumption driven by status anxiety is harming sustainability. How important is reducing consumption to stopping climate change? Is it possible to develop a society where status anxieties are reduced and, if so, what can politicians and campaigners do about it?

3. Wilkinson and Pickett suggest embedding economic democracy is key. How can this be achieved? Do their suggestions go far enough, or do they go too far? What can the experience of organisations that already have mutual or cooperative ownership structures teach us?

Please let us know what you think

Whatever view you take of the issues, we would very much like to hear about your discussion. Please send us a summary of your debate (perhaps 300 words) to debate@fabians.org.uk.

One nation in the world
A new foreign policy for the left

Edited by
**Marcus Roberts and
Ulrich Storck**

The world has changed dramatically since Labour last won power in 1997. While Labour has been has been gradually assembling domestic policy ideas under its 'one nation' banner, the party has not yet managed to find a compelling voice on global issues.

To present himself as a credible prime minister in waiting, Ed Miliband will need to craft a story which makes sense of the world in which he will govern, as well as an aspirational account of what a Labour government might seek to do. This collection of essays explores the choices, strategy and values that can guide the next Labour government as it seeks to addresses the challenges of a new global agenda.

With chapters by Olaf Boehnke, Ian Bond, Rachel Briggs, Malcolm Chalmers, David Clark, Rachael Jolley, Mark Leonard, Jessica Toale and Duncan Weldon.